We Need Librarians

by Jane Scoggins Bauld

Consulting Editor: Gail Saunders-Smith, Ph.D.

Consultant: Allison G. Kaplan, Coordinator, School Library Media Specialist Program, School of Education, University of Delaware

Pebble Books

an imprint of Capstone Press
Mankato, Minnesota

Pebble Books are published by Capstone Press
151 Good Counsel Drive, P.O. Box 669, Mankato, Minnesota 56002
http://www.capstone-press.com

Library of Congress Cataloging-in-Publication Data
Bauld, Jane Scoggins.
    We need librarians/by Jane Scoggins Bauld.
    p. cm.—(Helpers in our school)
    Includes bibliographical references and index.
    Summary: Simple text and photographs present librarians and their role in
elementary schools.
    ISBN 0-7368-0531-1
    1. School libraries—United States—Juvenile literature. 2. School librarians—
United States—Juvenile literature. [1. School librarians. 2. Librarians. 3. Occupations.]
I. Title. II. Series.
Z675.S3 B29   2000
027.8'0973—dc21   99-046868

Note to Parents and Teachers

The Helpers in Our School series supports national social studies
standards for how groups and institutions work to meet individual
needs. This book describes librarians and illustrates what they do in
school libraries. The photographs support early readers in
understanding the text. The repetition of words and phrases helps
early readers learn new words. This book also introduces early
readers to subject-specific vocabulary words, which are defined in
the Words to Know section. Early readers may need assistance to
read some words and to use the Table of Contents, Words to Know,
Read More, Internet Sites, and Index/Word List sections of the book.

Table of Contents

Librarians work in libraries.

Librarians talk with
teachers. Librarians
find out what students
are studying.

Librarians order materials for students to use. Some of the materials are books, magazines, and videos.

Librarians use computers
to catalog the materials.
Librarians put the materials
on library shelves.

Librarians read books to students.

14

Librarians teach students how to use libraries.

Librarians teach students how to search for information.

Librarians teach students where to find materials.

Librarians check out
materials to students.

Words to Know

catalog—to list and describe; librarians catalog all the materials in libraries; people use these lists to find information they need.

information—facts, ideas, and knowledge; people go to libraries to get information from books, newspapers, and other materials.

library—a place where materials are kept for reading or borrowing; many libraries have computers that people use to find information on the Internet.

materials—items that people may look at in libraries or check out of libraries; books, videos, magazines, and tapes are library materials.

order—to ask a business or store to send goods; librarians order new books and other materials for libraries.

Read More

Greene, Carol. *Librarians Help Us Find Information.* Chanhassen, Minn.: Child's World, 1999.

Munro, Roxie. *The Inside-Outside Book of Libraries.* New York: Dutton Children's Books, 1996.

Raatma, Lucia. *Libraries.* A True Book. New York: Children's Press, 1998.

Ready, Dee. *Librarians.* Community Helpers. Mankato, Minn.: Bridgestone Books, 1998.

Internet Sites

Become a Librarian!
http://www.becomealibrarian.com

Dewey Decimal System
http://tqjunior.thinkquest.org/5002

Jobs for Kids Who Like Reading
http://stats.bls.gov/k12/html/edu_read.htm

Index/Word List

books, 9, 13
catalog, 11
check out, 21
computers, 11
find, 19
information, 17
librarians, 5, 7, 9, 11,
  13, 15, 17, 19, 21
libraries, 5, 15
magazines, 9
materials, 9, 11,
  19, 21

order, 9
read, 13
search, 17
shelves, 11
students, 7, 9, 13, 15,
  17, 19, 21
studying, 7
teach, 15, 17, 19
teachers, 7
use, 9, 11, 15
videos, 9
work, 5

Word Count: 78
Early-Intervention Level: 13

Editorial Credits
Martha E. H. Rustad, editor; Abby Bradford, Bradfordesign, Inc., cover designer;
Kia Bielke, production designer; Kimberly Danger, photo researcher

Photo Credits
David F. Clobes, 8
Kim Stanton, 4, 10, 12
M & M Photography/Matt Swinden, 20
Marilyn Moseley LaMantia, 18
Unicorn Stock Photos/Jeff Greenberg, 14; Jean Higgins, 16
Uniphoto/Frank Siteman, cover; Llewellyn, 1
Visuals Unlimited/Jeff Greenberg, 6